Tell Me About Your GREATNESS!

By Sarah How, Psy. S.

Tell Me About Your GREATNESS!

ISBN 0-9893405-0-3

Publisher: How 2 Creative Services, 3220 18th Street South Suite 8C, Fargo, North Dakota 58104

Layout and design: Copyright © 2013, How 2 Creative Services of Fargo, North Dakota

Heart art on front cover provided by Justin How and used with permission.

Several original photographs provided by Mrs. Mikayla Doeden and used with permission.

Author photograph by CK Photography of Sartell, Minnesota

All children included in the photographs were from Mrs. Mikayla Doeden's 2011-2012 Kindergarten class at C.A. Lodoen Kindergarten Center in West Fargo, North Dakota. Children were photographed with parent permission.

Many thanks to the people who have touched my life with their greatness.

How to make the most of this book

As adults, we have the power in our words and actions to recognise and celebrate what is right in children. We are each given messages about who we are by the words people speak to us, positive or negative. Each of us can choose to use our own words to celebrate the positive we see in others. It has been a journey for me, as a school psychologist and mother, to shift my thinking and to start seeing and naming all the positive attributes I see in the children around me every day. I was inspired to do this as I learned the Nurtured Heart Approach®, created by Howard Glasser. Although positivity is important for change, it is only one part of this approach.

You can use this book as a starting point for conversations on character. If you are an educator, you can introduce 'greatness lessons', using this book to bring this way of seeing and speaking to life. Such lessons can teach children the idea that 'greatness' is available to everyone, not just a select few. As you teach each page, you can foster discussions that will soon brim with specific examples of how your pupils have shown and are showing these character qualities. As children learn to see what is right rather than what is going wrong, they begin to express greatness themselves and evoke it in others. This helps shift the classroom climate to the energy of positivity. You can hold 'greatness meetings' at the close of day to end with positivity and gratitude as the children have the opportunity to recognise character qualities they have observed during the day.

I encourage you to use this book and your own creativity to ignite a passion for seeing what is right in children. Classroom and school culture is central to learning. Expanding positivity in your classroom or home in concrete and specific ways helps all children grow emotionally stronger. And I'd love to hear how you've used this book to do it.

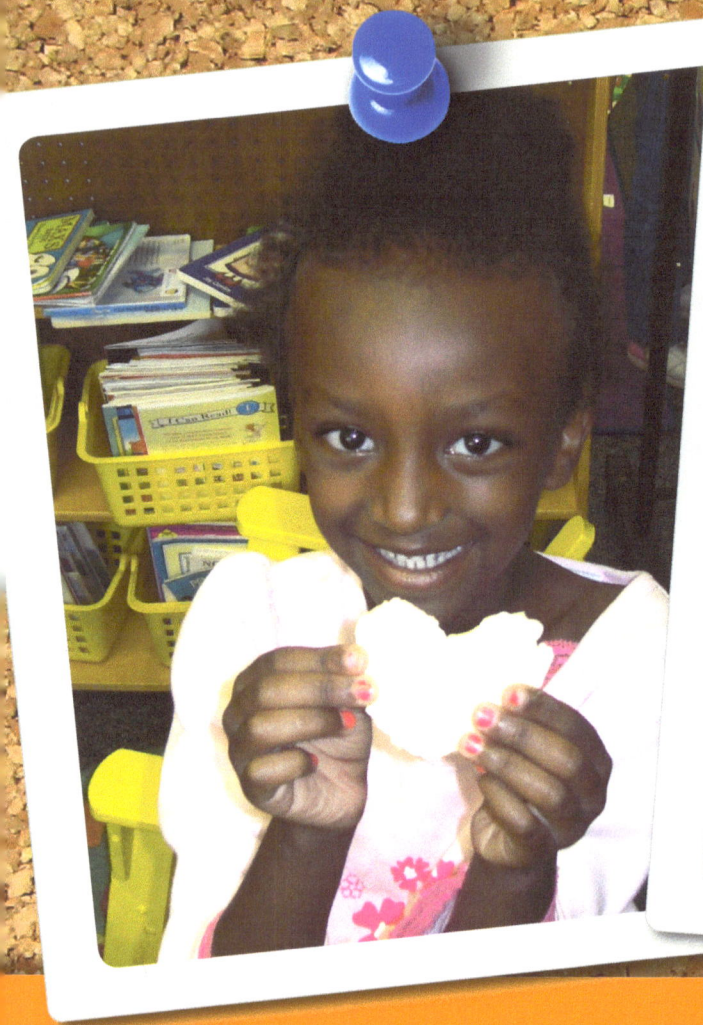

Greatness

I show my greatness by using my eyes to see and my words to say what is right about who I am and what I do.

I am Full of GREATNESS!

Kind

I show my greatness by caring for all, no matter their skin colour, eye colour, body shape or size, clothes they wear or language they speak.

I am KIND!

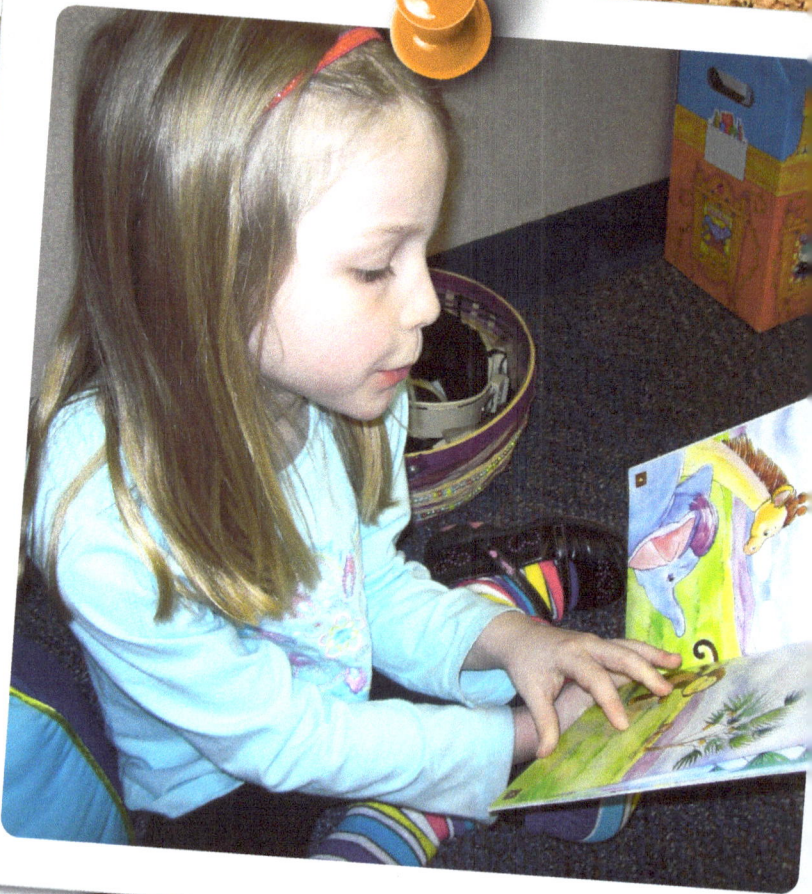

Focused

I show my greatness by looking with my eyes
and keeping my thoughts on school work.

I am FOCUSED!

Energetic

I show my greatness by making healthy choices of running, climbing, jumping and swinging on the playground.

I am ENERGETIC!

7

Independent

I show my greatness by doing my school
work and reading all by myself.

I am INDEPENDENT!

Organised

I show my greatness by putting my school
things in my desk where they belong.

I am ORGANISED!

Friendly

I show my greatness by playing nicely and including everyone.

I am FRIENDLY!

unique

I show my greatness by knowing there is only one me
and celebrating that by being the best me I can be.

I am UNIQUE!

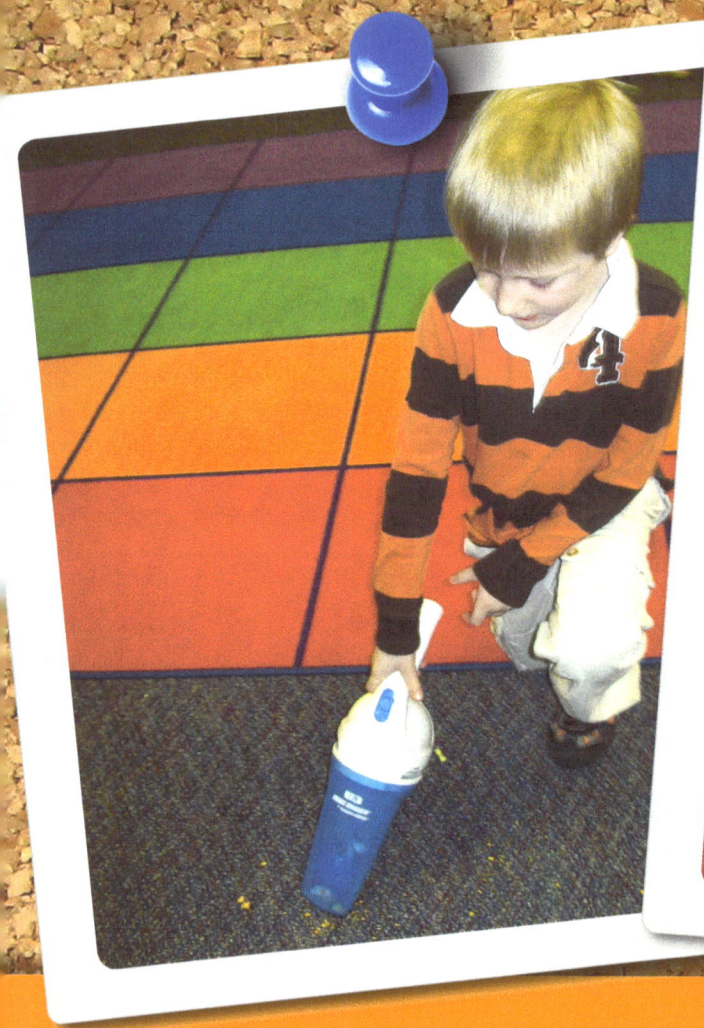

Helpful

I show my greatness by helping to keep our classroom tidy.

I am HELPFUL!

Joyful

I show my greatness by sharing the smile on my face and the happiness in my heart with everyone.

I am JOYFUL!

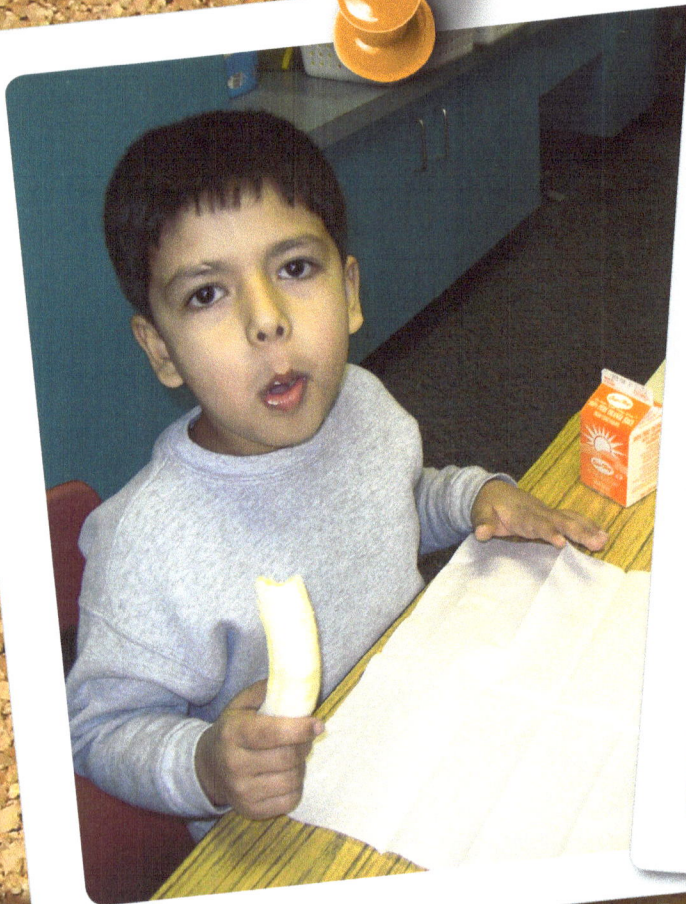

Healthy and Safe

I show my greatness by eating healthy foods and washing my hands so I do not spread germs.

I am HEALTHY and SAFE!

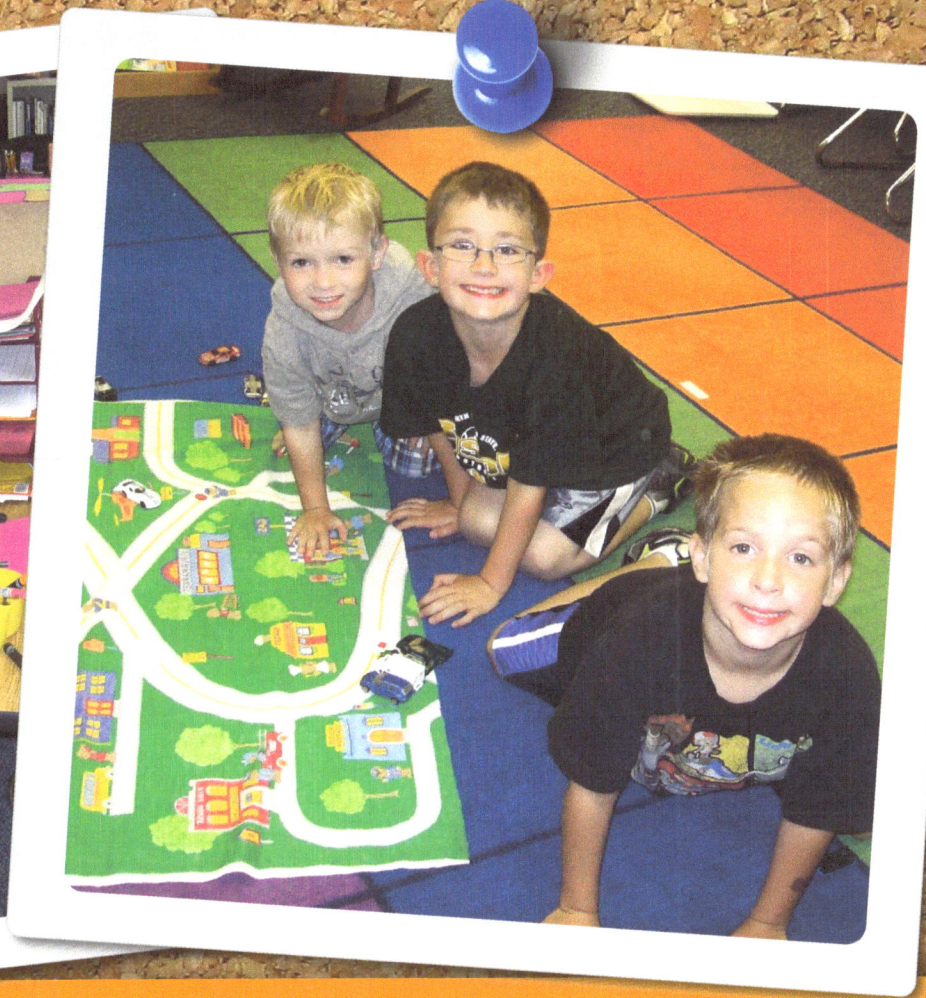

cooperative

I show my greatness by playing, sharing
and taking turns with my friends.

I am COOPERATIVE!

Creative

I show my greatness by drawing, painting and creating new things.

I am CREATIVE!

Patient

I show my greatness by quietly putting my hand
up and waiting for the teacher to ask me.

I am PATIENT!

Responsible

I show my greatness by starting straight away when it is time to tidy up.

I am RESPONSIBLE!

Determined

I show my greatness by never giving up, even when it is difficult.

I am DETERMINED!

Imaginative

I show my greatness by dreaming of becoming
a builder, a parent, a teacher or a superhero.

I am IMAGINATIVE!

Self-Control

I show my greatness by walking in a line, staying in my own space and keeping my hands, feet and unkind words to myself.

I am full of SELF-CONTROL!

Learner

I show my greatness by looking with
my eyes and listening with my ears.

I am a LEARNER!

Greatness

We have shown you what Greatness looks like.

Now it's your turn to let your greatness shine bright.

You are FULL of GREATNESS!

Every school day

is an opportunity to embrace and honour what is right in children. School is a great place to recognise children verbally for all the amazing character qualities they show, like kindness, patience, organisation etc. This book is designed to teach children to recognise their own voices in seeing what is right in themselves and others. For educators, this is part of the 'hidden curriculum' within education that can't be pulled off a shelf as a book, but needs to be spoken and seen throughout the school day. Children learn to give themselves evidence of their own 'greatness' that is a true reflection of their many character qualities. Every evidence given and every moment celebrated helps children grow strong on the inside. Today is the day to start asking children, 'Tell me about your greatness!' and teaching them ways to look at the ordinary as extraordinary.

About the author

Sarah How lives with her husband and four children in Fargo, North Dakota. Their family is blended with two of their children being adopted from foster care. Sarah graduated from Minnesota State University Moorhead with her Specialist in School Psychology. She is in her 15th year as a Nationally Certified School Psychologist with West Fargo Public Schools in West Fargo, North Dakota. She is a Certified Nurtured Heart Approach® Specialist providing speaking, training and consultation in The Nurtured Heart Approach®.

A personal note

'Tell me about your greatness!' are the words I used to greet our four children after school and focus on the things they had done right throughout their school day. At first awkward, it soon became a way for us to connect and focus on the good stuff. All this was the beginning of our family learning to embrace The Nurtured Heart Approach®. Beautifully, this intentional way of living did not just stay at home. As a practising school psychologist, I found the approach to be powerful in teaching children and educators to create meaningful relationships and intentional interactions - emotional nutrition for the heart.

The Nurtured Heart Approach® was created by Howard Glasser.
For more information visit www.ChildrensSuccessFoundation.com.

From teacher to teacher

In a changing world, we need to create a place where children are accepted and taught about their greatness. Teaching children to grow strong on the inside is critical to their well-being and growth as a human. In our classroom we notice what is right about each other, rather than what is wrong in the moment. It provides just the right balance between establishing clear rules and positively recognising all children in our classroom. As a class, we absolutely refuse to reward negativity. We are constantly modelling how to show our greatness by doing our best, and being leaders by following the rules. Sometimes we need to take a break to refresh ourselves and get back on track to our greatness.

Mrs. Mikayla Doeden
Kindergarten Teacher

A message from Alastair Gardiner

Alastair Gardiner
Director of the
Nurtured Heart Approach UK

Sarah How is a woman of amazing substance and integrity who has dedicated herself to identifying and creating greatness in everybody she meets. The beauty of 'Tell Me About your Greatness' is its simplicity, encouraging children and adults to clear away the mist of day to day life and really recognise what stunning attributes we all display on a second by second, minute by minute basis. Identifying this greatness, no matter how small, enriches relationships creating the inner wealth that can only propel children towards continuing success and a life full of light. Through her books and professional practice Sarah continues to demonstrate that she can truly help parents and teachers connect with that instinctive desire to support children in living their lives to their full potential.

If you are wanting more information about the Nurtured Heart Approach® in the UK please contact:

www.nurturedheartapproachuk.com
Nurtured Heart Approach UK
2nd Floor, Station House
Stamford New Road,
Altrincham. Cheshire. WA14 1EP
Email – alastair@nhauk.com

25

Kind

Energetic

Helpful

Focused

Patient

GREAT

Healthy and Safe

Creative

Joyful

cooperative

Organised Friendly

Unique

Independent Learner

NESS!

Imaginative

Responsible

Determined Self-Control

9 780989 340502